BUGS
FROM
HEAD TO TAIL

WRITTEN BY **Stacey Roderick**

ILLUSTRATED BY **Kwanchai Moriya**

Kids Can Press

What bug has a head like this?

A rhinoceros beetle!

One look at the horn jutting out of the male rhinoceros beetle's head and it's easy to see how it got its name! The male uses its rhino-like horn for fighting other males and for pushing through leafy litter on the ground to escape danger. In fact, this superstrong creature can use its fierce-looking horn to lift up to 850 times its own weight!

What bug has
antennae like this?

A luna moth!

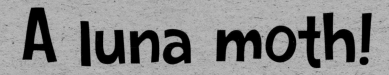

The luna moth uses its two feathery-looking antennae for finding its way and for smelling. The male luna moth's antennae are wider. bushier and more sensitive than the female's. This helps the male smell the special chemicals (called pheromones) that the female sends out when it's time to reproduce. or have babies.

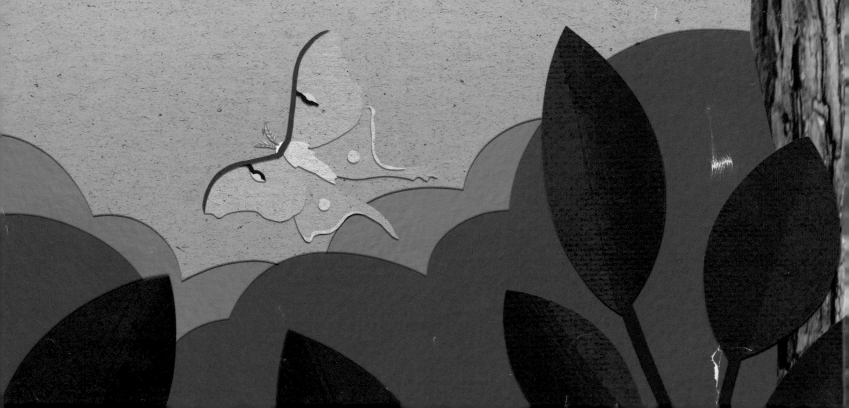

What bug has
eyes like this?

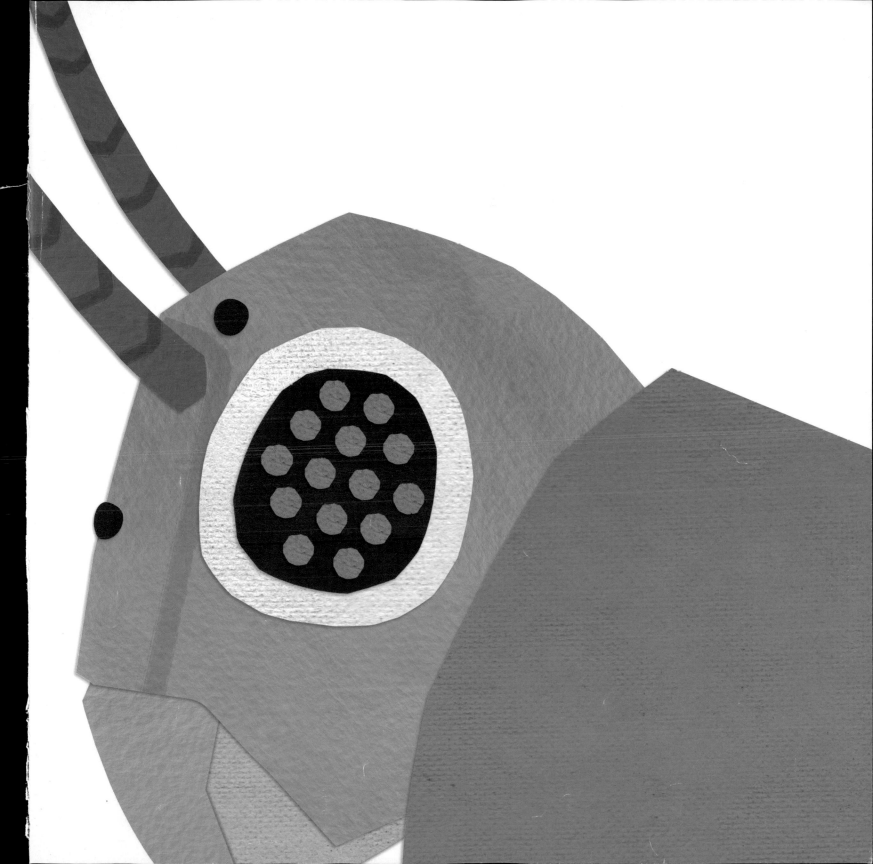

A grasshopper!

A grasshopper's two large compound eyes are easy to spot — but look closer! In between, there are also three much smaller simple eyes. The bulging compound eyes are made up of thousands of tiny lenses, each one sitting at a slightly different angle. This allows the grasshopper to see a wide area without having to turn its head. Its simple eyes have one lens each (just like human eyes) and are used for sensing light.

What bug has
a body like this?

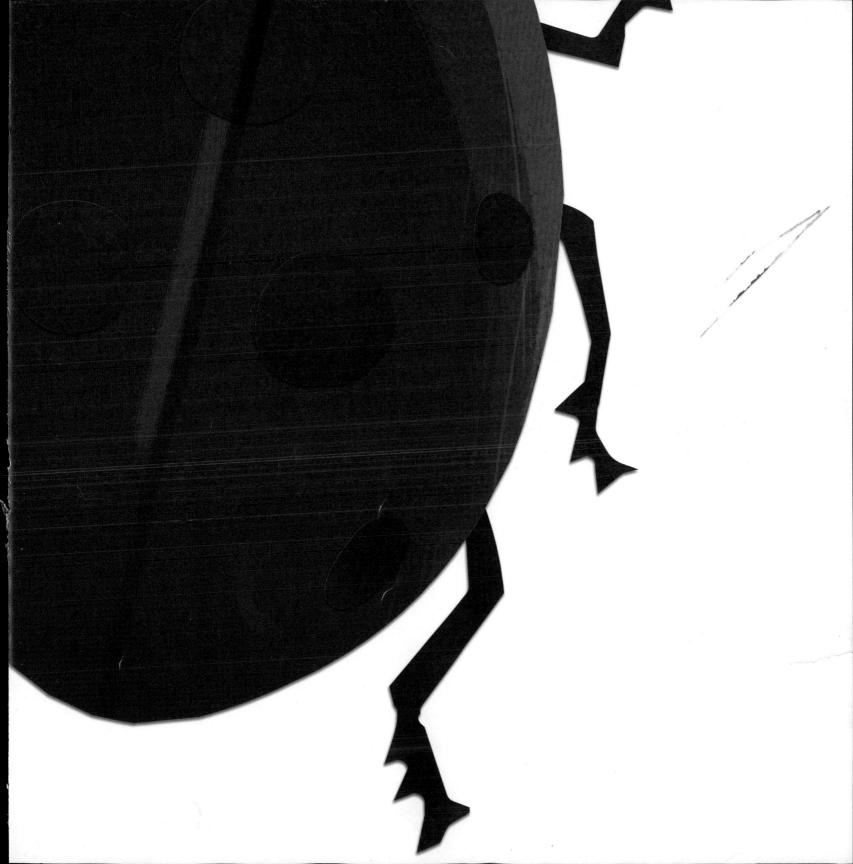

A ladybug!

This brightly colored beetle can have anywhere from two to twenty spots depending on which species, or type, of ladybug it is. A ladybug has a set of tough outer wings that act like a suit of armor to protect its soft body. These wings are part of the ladybug's exoskeleton, or "outside skeleton." (A second set of wings for flying is tucked underneath.)

What bug has wings like this?

A monarch butterfly!

Thousands of tiny, overlapping scales make up the orange and black markings on the monarch's wings. This pattern isn't just beautiful — it's also a warning to stay away. The monarch butterfly tastes *awful* to would-be predators (animals that want to eat it). That's because during its caterpillar stage, before it turns into a butterfly, the monarch feeds only on milkweed. These plants contain toxins, or poisons, that stay in the butterfly's body its entire life.

What bug has hair like this?

A tarantula!

Even though most people don't think of bugs as hairy animals, lots of them are! In fact, the tarantula spider is known for being *very* hairy. Many tarantula species have thick, wiry bristles that act as protection. The special prickly hairs fall out very easily and are painful when they get into a predator's eyes or mouth. These tarantulas can even use their hind legs to flick hair from their bellies at an attacker!

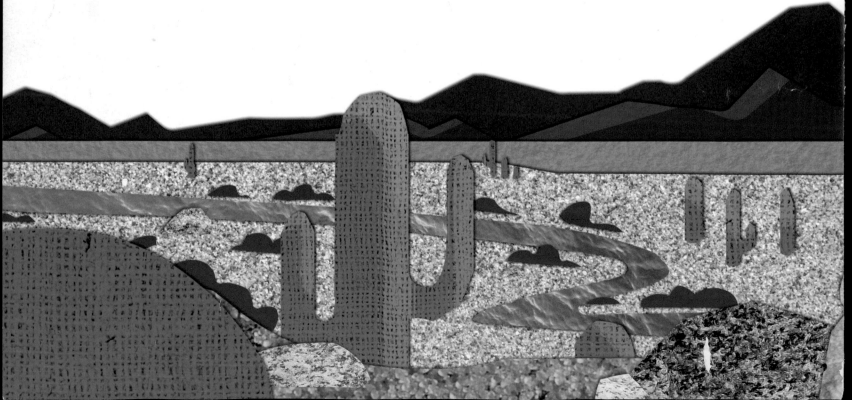

What bug has legs like this?

A millipede!

The millipede belongs to a group of bugs whose name means "many legs." A millipede's long body is protected by a strong exoskeleton made up of segments, or sections. Each segment has two pairs of legs, and altogether a millipede might have up to 750 legs! But even with all these legs, the millipede isn't very fast. It *is* very good at using its many legs to burrow, or dig, into the ground, though.

What bug has a *tail* like this?

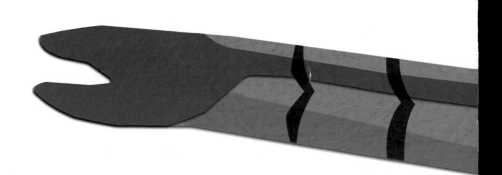

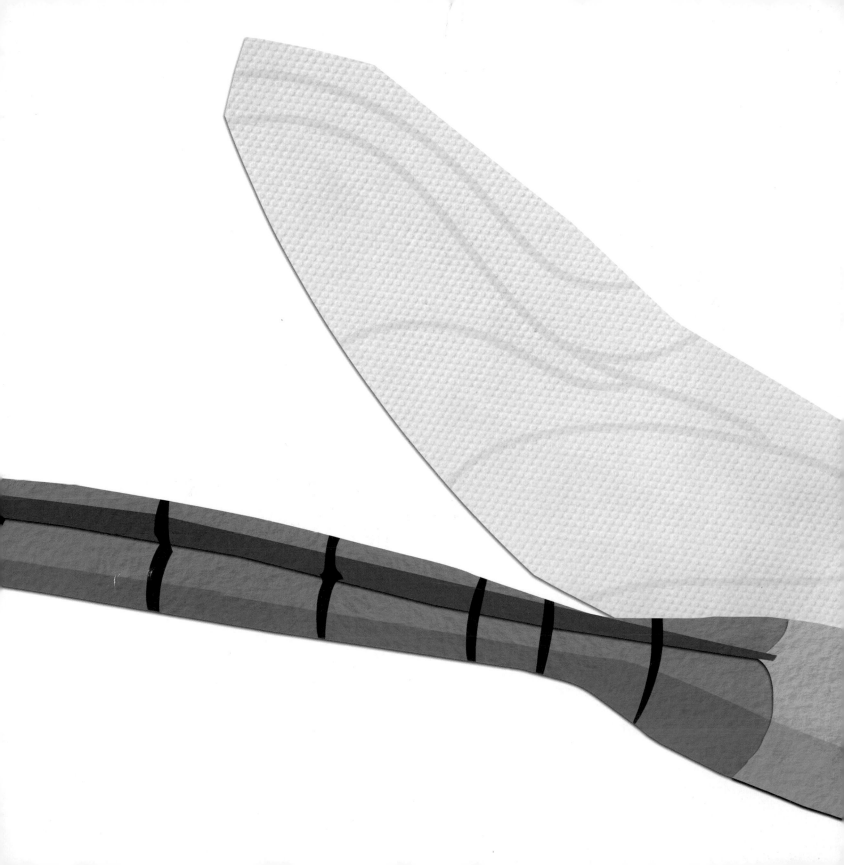

None!

A true tail grows out of an animal's spine, and no bug has a spine! What might look like a tail on this dragonfly is actually a very long, thin abdomen — the body part that contains its stomach and other important organs. A dragonfly's abdomen is made up of ten segments and can move up and down, which is why it is sometimes confused for a wagging tail.

Other Awesome Bugs

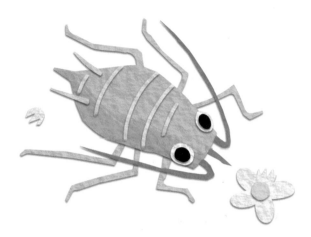

The aphid has long mouthparts for sucking juice from plants.

The jumping spider has four pairs of eyes.

The leaf-cutter ant has "elbowed," or bent, antennae.

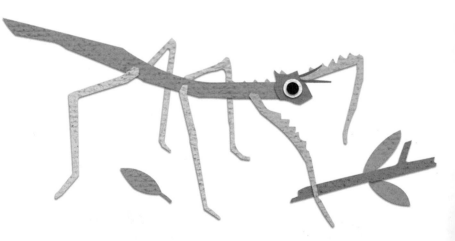

A stick insect's body is perfect for hiding among plants and trees.

A bumblebee collects pollen using the hairs on its legs.

The spots on an owl butterfly's wings look like pygmy owl eyes.

The praying mantis has small hooks on its front legs for trapping food.

A Bit More about Bugs

The creatures we call bugs in this book all belong to a very large group of animals with the scientific name "arthropod." Arthropods are invertebrates (animals without a backbone) that have exoskeletons and jointed legs. Arthropods include smaller groups of animals, such as insects, arachnids and myriapods. One way to tell these groups apart is by counting their legs: insects have six legs, arachnids have eight legs and myriapods have more than eight legs.

For Owen, my love bug — S.R.

For Shannon and Jina, because where would I bee without you? — K.M.

Acknowledgments

Many thanks to Professor Sandy M. Smith, University of Toronto,
and Dr. Christopher Darling, Senior Curator of Insects, Royal Ontario Museum,
for generously sharing their time and expertise to review this manuscript.
Any errors that may have crept in along the way are solely mine.
And, of course, much gratitude to all the very talented people at KCP,
with special thanks to Yvette Ghione, Olga Kidisevic, Julia Naimska and
Katie Scott. Finally, an enormous thank you to Kwanchai Moriya
for all his extraordinary illustrations.

Kids Can Press gratefully acknowledges the financial support of the Government of Ontario, through the Ontario Media Development Corporation; the Ontario Arts Council; the Canada Council for the Arts; and the Government of Canada, through the CBF, for our publishing activity.

Published in Canada and the U.S. by Kids Can Press Ltd.
25 Dockside Drive, Toronto, ON M5A 0B5

Kids Can Press is a Corus Entertainment Inc. company

www.kidscanpress.com

The artwork in this book was created in Adobe Photoshop and Illustrator, using original photographs and textures.

The text is set in Squidtoonz.

Edited by Katie Scott
Designed by Julia Naimska

Printed and bound in Shenzhen, China, in 3/2017 by Imago

CM 17 0 9 8 7 6 5 4 3 2 1

Library and Archives Canada Cataloguing in Publication

Roderick, Stacey, author
    Bugs from head to tail / Stacey Roderick ; Kwanchai Moriya, illustrator.

(Head to tail ; 3)

ISBN 978-1-77138-729-3 (hardback)

    1. Insects—Juvenile literature. I. Moriya, Kwanchai, illustrator II. Title.

QL467.2.R63 2017   j595.7   C2016-906699-1